MAKING SANTA

by Susan Bonser

Making Santa
An Exploration of DALL•E2 and AI

ISBN: 9798386224790
Imprint: Independently published

This is an AI exploration in the creation of realistic images of men dressed as Santa Claus. The images in this book were generated using natural language digital AI tool DALL-E2 then retouched and prepped for publication using Adobe Photoshop and InDesign. Any resemblance to real persons or previously published characters is purely coincidental and unintentional. Adobe Acrobat was used in the print production workflow. Some of the text was generated using ChatGPT then edited by the author in Microsoft Word.

Other books we have produced using AI:
Making Faces and *Making Faces2*
You can email us at pennjournaloel@gmail.com.
See our other publications at http://thebonsers.com
All content © 2023 Susan Bonser

Contents

About DALL·E2 *(ChatGPT)*

History of the image of Santa Claus *(ChatGPT)*

Prompts and results

Enhancing the prompt

Refining the prompt

Inpainting edits

Variations

Variations: series

External software edits

Full figure Santa

Another prompt strategy

Outpainting vs. Photoshop

Prep for printing or digital distribution

Oops!

About DALL·E2

In January 2021, OpenAI unveiled their latest artificial intelligence (AI) model, DALL-E2. This model is a successor to their earlier model, DALL-E, which was released in 2020. DALL-E2 has taken the internet by storm, with its ability to generate incredibly realistic images from text descriptions.

What is DALL-E2?

DALL-E2 is an AI model that is trained to generate images from text descriptions. It uses a combination of techniques from computer vision and natural language processing to create images that match the input text as closely as possible.

The model is named after Salvador Dali, the famous Spanish surrealist artist, and Pixar's WALL-E, the beloved robot protagonist of the movie of the same name. The name reflects the model's ability to generate surreal and imaginative images from textual input.

How does DALL-E2 work?

DALL-E2 works by using a technique called a transformer network. This is a type of neural network that is commonly used in natural language processing tasks. The transformer network can process sequential data, such as text, and generate a set of feature vectors that represent the input.

Once the transformer network has processed the text, it is passed through a separate image generation network. This network takes the feature vectors as input and generates an image that matches the text description as closely as possible.

What can DALL-E2 do?

DALL-E2 can generate a wide range of images, from realistic depictions of everyday objects to surreal and imaginative scenes. Some examples of images that have been generated by the model include a snail made of harpsichords, a computer keyboard made of waffles, and a teapot made of giraffes.

One of the most impressive things about DALL-E2 is its ability to generate images that are not only visually impressive but also semantically coherent. This means that the images it generates make sense in the context of the input text.

For example, if you give DALL-E2 the input text "an armchair in the shape of an avocado," it will generate an image that looks like an armchair, but with the shape and texture of an avocado. This level of semantic coherence is what sets DALL-E2 apart from other image generation models.

Why is DALL-E2 important?

DALL-E2 is important because it represents a major advancement in AI image generation technology. It has the potential to be used in a wide range of applications, from art and design to advertising and e-commerce.

For example, an artist could use DALL-E2 to quickly generate a set of images to accompany a text description of their work. A designer could use the model to generate images of furniture or interior design concepts for their clients. An e-commerce company could use DALL-E2 to generate product images that are more visually appealing and unique than traditional photographs.

Conclusion

DALL-E2 is an impressive AI model that has the potential to revolutionize the way we generate and use images. Its ability to generate semantically coherent images from text descriptions is a major step forward in AI image generation technology. As the technology continues to improve, we can expect to see DALL-E2 and similar models used in a wide range of applications, from art and design to advertising and e-commerce.

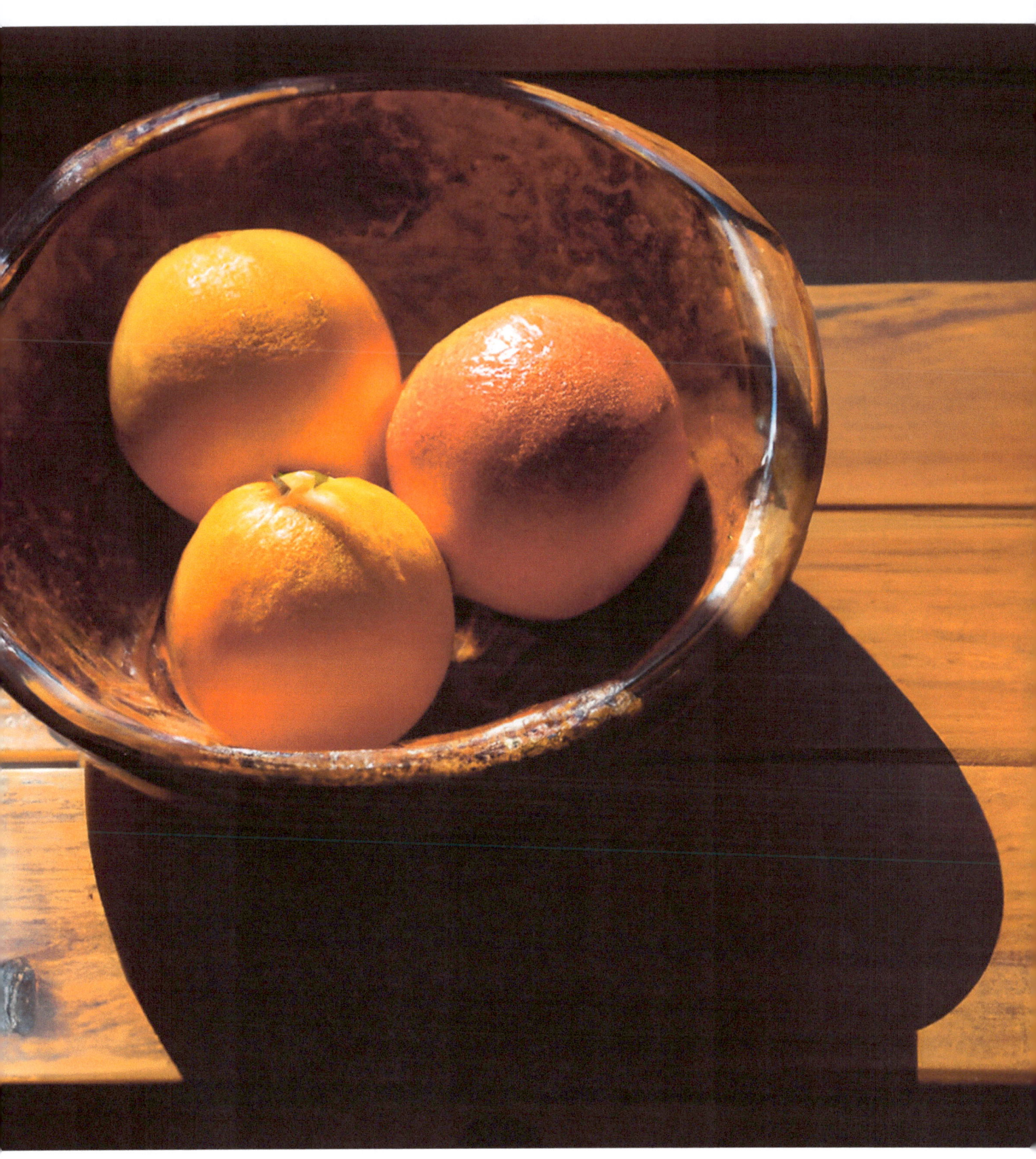

My early experiment. PROMPT: Closeup from overhead of fresh oranges and a grapefruit in a rustic hand-hewn wooden bowl on a wood table by a window with sunlight streaming in.

History of the visual image of Santa Claus

The visual image of Santa Claus, with his round belly, white beard, and red suit, is one of the most recognizable figures in popular culture. Children around the world eagerly anticipate his annual visit, leaving out milk and cookies in hopes of catching a glimpse of the jolly old man. But where did this beloved character come from, and how did he become the icon we know today?

The origins of Santa Claus can be traced back to Saint Nicholas, a fourth-century bishop in the Greek town of Myra. Saint Nicholas was known for his generosity, particularly towards children, and he became a popular figure in Christian folklore. His feast day, celebrated on December 6th, was associated with gift-giving, and over time, the tradition of giving gifts to children on this day spread throughout Europe.

In the 16th century, the Protestant Reformation led to a decline in the celebration of Saint Nicholas' feast day in many parts of Europe. However, the popularity of the gift-giving tradition persisted, and in some regions, it merged with other winter festivals, such as the Roman Saturnalia and the Germanic Yule, to create a new holiday celebration.

In the 18th century, this holiday celebration began to take on a more secular character, with the figure of Saint Nicholas becoming increasingly associated with Christmas. The image of Santa Claus as we know him today began to take shape in the United States in the early 19th century, thanks in large part to the influence of popular culture.

One of the most influential figures in the development of the modern Santa Claus was the political cartoonist Thomas Nast. In the 1860s, Nast began drawing a series of illustrations for Harper's Weekly that depicted Santa Claus as a plump, bearded man in a red suit. Nast's illustrations helped to popularize the image of Santa Claus and cemented his place as a fixture of the Christmas season.

Other cultural icons also helped to shape the image of Santa Claus. The poem "A Visit from St. Nicholas," also known as "The Night Before Christmas," was first published anonymously in 1823 and quickly became a holiday classic. The poem's description of Santa Claus as "a right jolly old elf" who "had a broad face and a little round belly" helped to solidify the image of Santa Claus as a jolly, rotund figure.

In the early 20th century, the image of Santa Claus continued to evolve. The Coca-Cola Company, in particular, played a major role in shaping the modern visual image of Santa Claus. In the 1930s, the company began using Santa Claus in its holiday advertising campaigns, depicting him as a plump, rosy-cheeked figure in a bright red suit. The popularity of these ads helped to solidify the image of Santa Claus as we know him today.

Today, Santa Claus is one of the most beloved figures of the holiday season, and his image can be found everywhere from billboards to shopping malls to children's books. While the origins of Santa Claus may be rooted in Christian tradition, his current image owes much to the influence of popular culture and the marketing efforts of corporations like Coca-Cola. Despite this commercialization, however, the spirit of generosity and goodwill that Saint Nicholas embodied still remains at the heart of the holiday season.

Right, Using the descriptive words found in this ChatGPT-generated history of Santa, DALL•E2 returned this happy fellow.

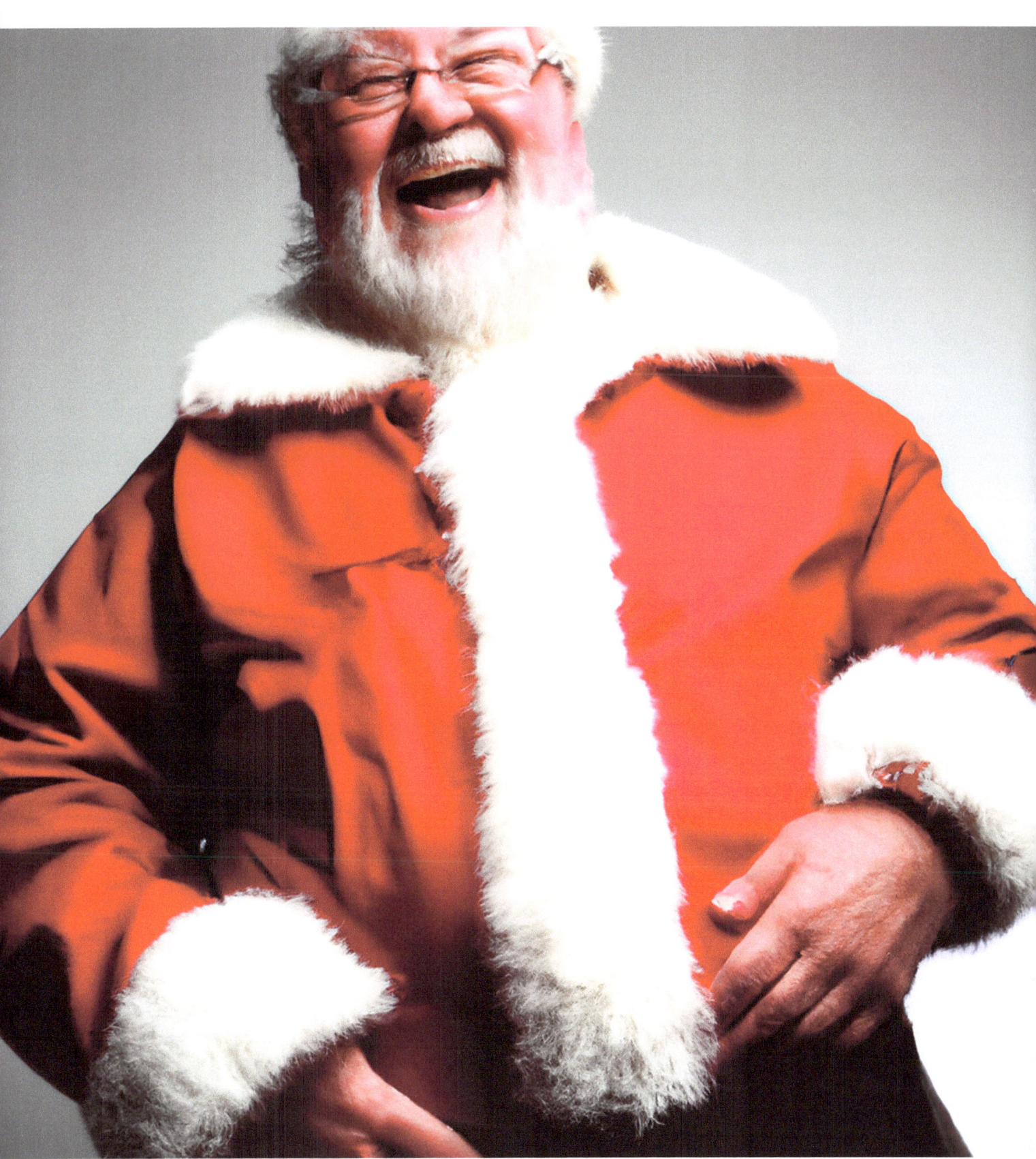

PROMPT: Dramatic studio lighting of a beautiful jolly old man with a white beard, round belly and red suit laughing.

Prompts and results

The key to unlocking the magic of Dall•E2 is the words you use. There may be no right words or wrong words (though there are strict acceptability guidelines), but there are many theories floating around about words to use to get the best results. It's important to understand, however, that using the exact same words again will not result in the same images—or perhaps not even in the same quality of images. So, there are some other factors affecting how well my prompt achieves a good response.

And this is where we all stand. On the other side of the curtain, randomly trying out this word and that to get an image we like. It is nearly impossible to imagine an image in your head, then describe it as a prompt and have Dall•E2 return your vision in spectacular Technicolor. What pops up is always a surprise. Very often it is a really nice surprise and an image that is workable.

I found it was better to work Dall•E2 along, like clay. As you can see, a simple prompt such as "Close-up of Santa" resulted in a photographic image of what seems to be vintage plastic blow molds. A much more detailed prompt results in an interesting image and a man dressed in Indian or Middle Eastern style clothing. I found that if I did not specify ethnicity in my prompt, I often received a mix. The same is true of gender. If I didn't specify, I got a mix. Even if specified, I sometimes got a surprising mix.

In future versions, there may be better ways to connect with the program to help it understand what the user wants, what the user is imagining. Either it has to be trained or the user has to be trained. Right now, Dall•E2 is an amazing tool, but what it is producing is more Dall•E than me. I am definitely contributing, but I am a string tied to a runaway balloon. It is a bumpy ride.

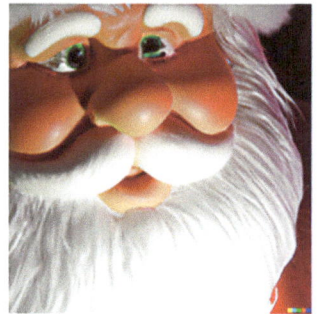
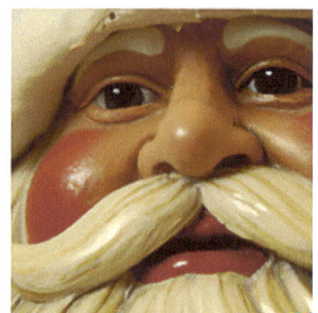
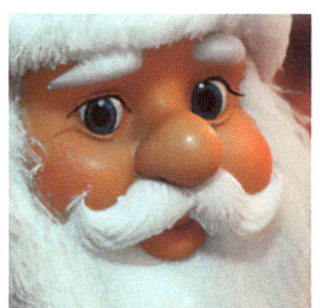
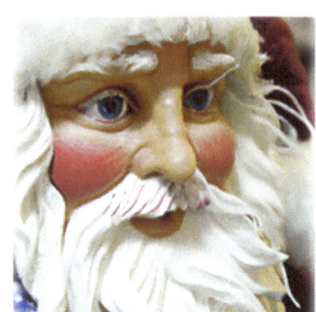

PROMPT: Closeup of Santa Claus.

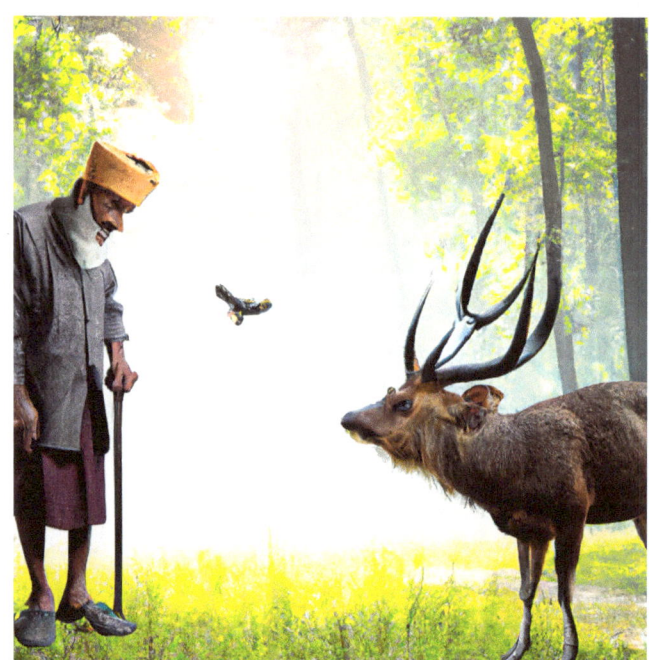

PROMPT: High resolution photograph that is full figure of an old man and a buck deer standing in sunny woods.

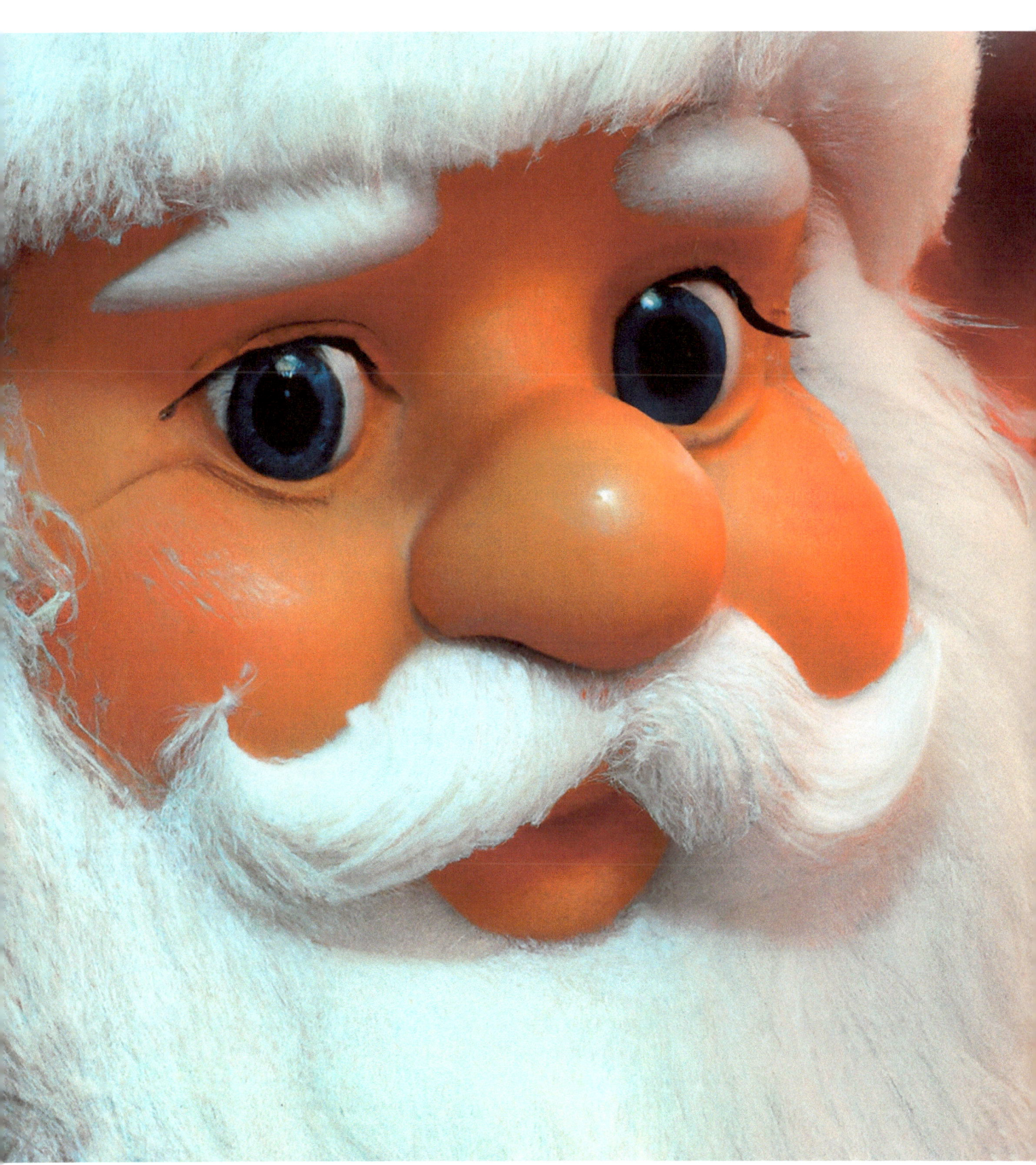

PROMPT: Closeup of Santa Claus.

Enhancing the prompt

My prompts included photographic terms, lighting descriptors, backgrounds, as well as clear descriptions of the subjects. Some words didn't get good results. "Kindly" was one word that was not reflected in the character of the images it generated, for instance.

Having had a couple of scary Santa Claus experiences as a young child, I was very picky about the personality that my Santa image choices portrayed. Dalle•E2 did not exhibit any innate understanding of the character of an acceptable Santa and returned images of men looking grumpy, derelict and downright terrifying. By keeping at it, and generating a lot of images (more than 50), I eventually came to a few that I felt comfortable being alone in the same room with. And would put on the cover of a book.

Words like chubby, tousled and ruddy resulted in appropriate responses. I found that the first generation, though, was only the start. I had to work the image with edits in the program and externally to get to the result I envisioned.

I tried uploading a picture of my husband, letting Dall•E2 turn him into Santa, but the results were even scarier than the Santa images I generated directly with Dall•E2. I abandoned that track immediately.

Dall•E2 was forgiving of incorrect usage of language and often returned the characteristic even if grammatically incorrect or misspelled. In long prompts, it often ignored words and did not return those characteristics. This may not be true, but in long prompts it seemed like the words closer to the start of the prompt were more likely reflected in the image than those at the end of the prompt. Because of that, I concentrated on achieving the character of the person I wanted to portray Santa and left the background and costume prompts until later in the process when I had a person.

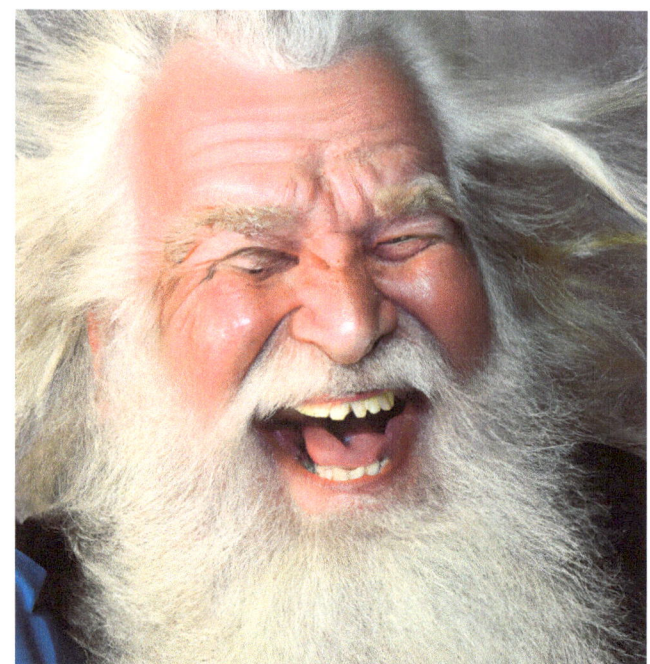

PROMPT: Closeup of a happy blue-eyed eighty-year-old chubby old man with tousled pure white curly hair, long pure white beard, pure white eyebrows and a ruddy complexion laughing.

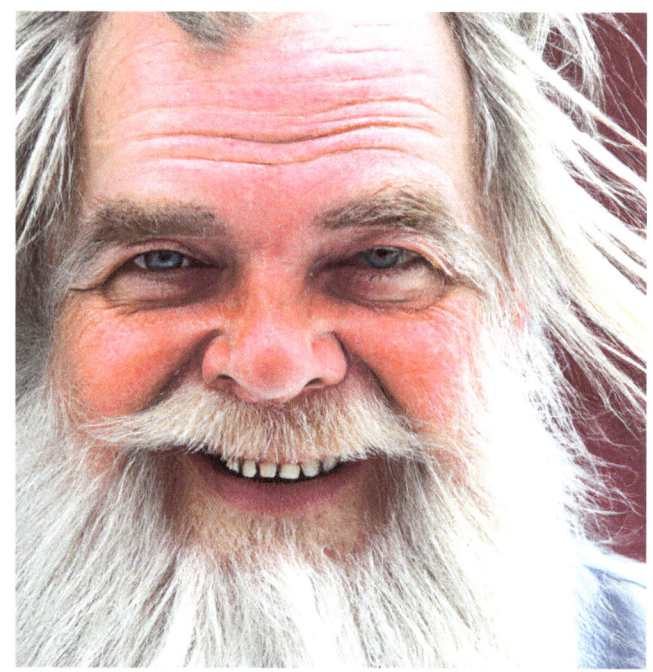

PROMPT: Closeup of a seventy year old chubby man with tousled white hair, white beard, white eyebrows and a ruddy complexion smiling.

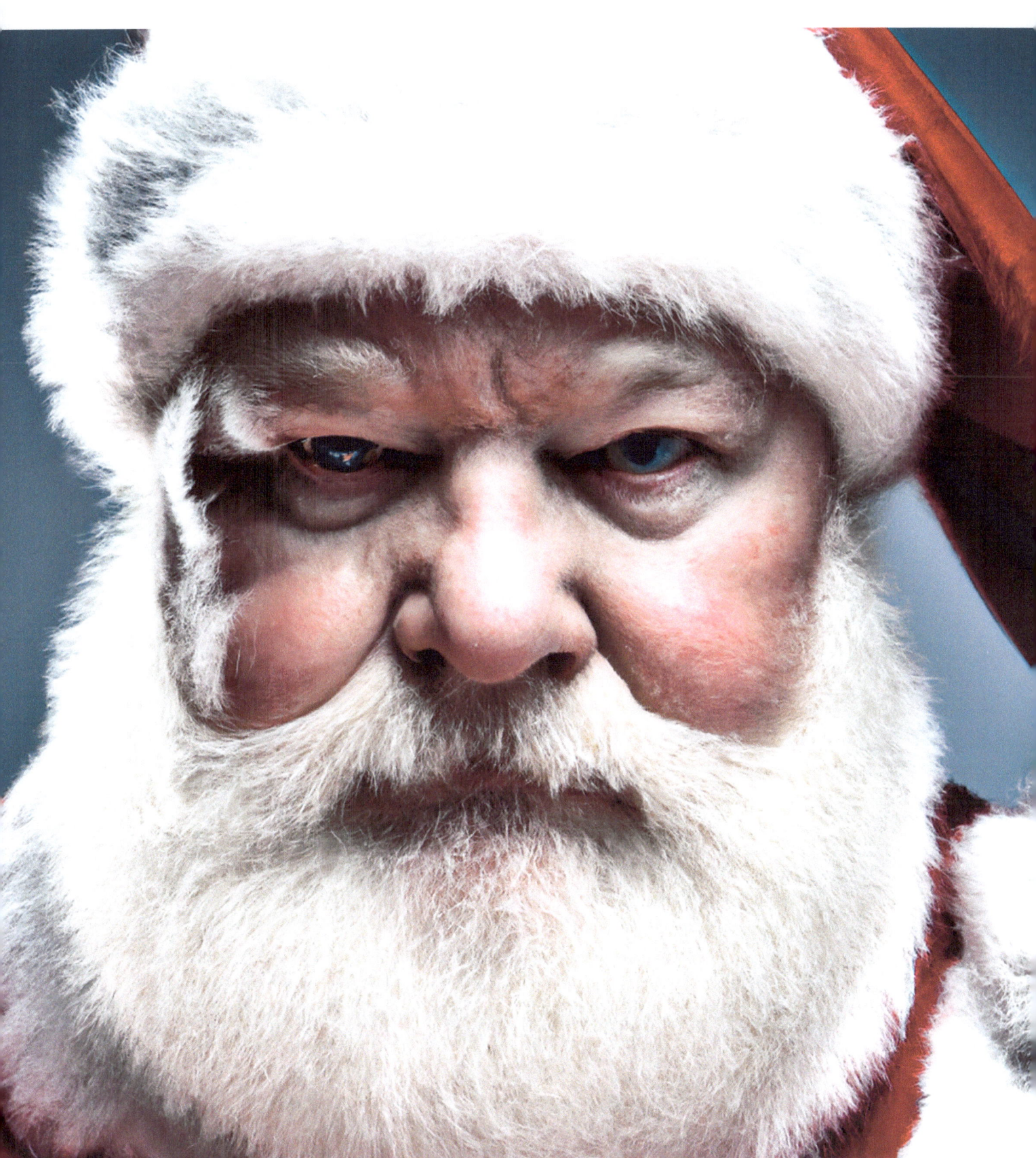
PROMPT: Closeup photo of old man who looks like Santa Claus.

Refining the prompt

The more specific the words of the prompt, the better the chance of having that characteristic accurately reflected in the image generation. You can see I specified eye color, pure white hair, beard and eyebrows. Logically, when I did not, I got brown eyes and all colors of hair.

I chose a couple of my favorite images and tried editing to move them closer to my vision. Sometimes with the Dall•E2 editing tools, it was just better to go on to another image or start again with a new generation. Editing was not always an improvement.

This was my first Santa choice. In his first generation, he had some problems with his eyes that I chose not to correct within Dall•E2. He also had some teeth problems—pointy, yellow teeth. I did correct that using the Dall•E2 edit tool.

I found eye problems and teeth problems were very common in photographic portrait style image generation in Dall•E2. Some faces were generated with two rows of teeth, incorrect teeth, broken or missing teeth or yellow teeth. Eyes were frequently constructed poorly—not anatomically correct. Some looked like lizard eyes or cats' eyes. Eyes were sometimes looking in different directions or popping out of their sockets.

I had my heart set on bushy eyebrows and a colorful background. I will explain how I achieved those things. There is most certainly no one right way to get to the image you want. I am simply demonstrating how I, personally, got to where I ended up. I am fascinated to read about other people's processes and thought mine might be useful as well.

The really interesting thing is that this will all most likely be moot as the succeeding generations of this tool are developed and released. Perhaps it will be able to be trained. Maybe it will just become so culturally literate it will read our minds.

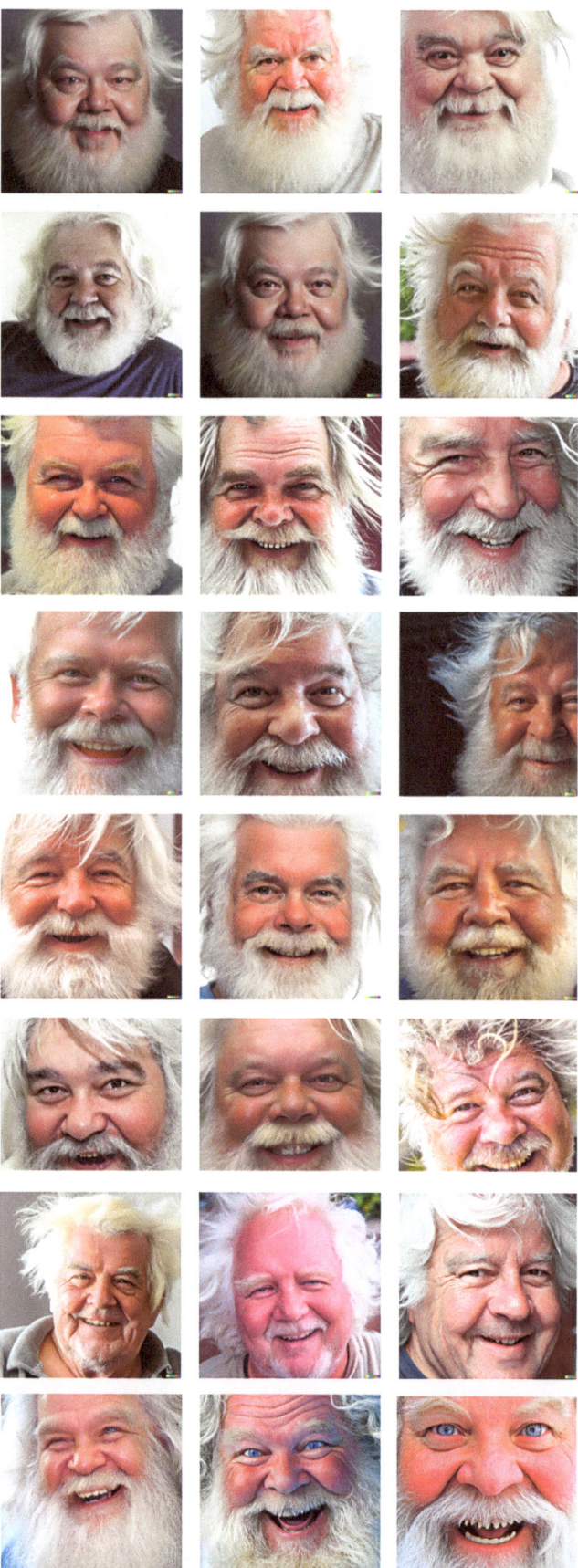

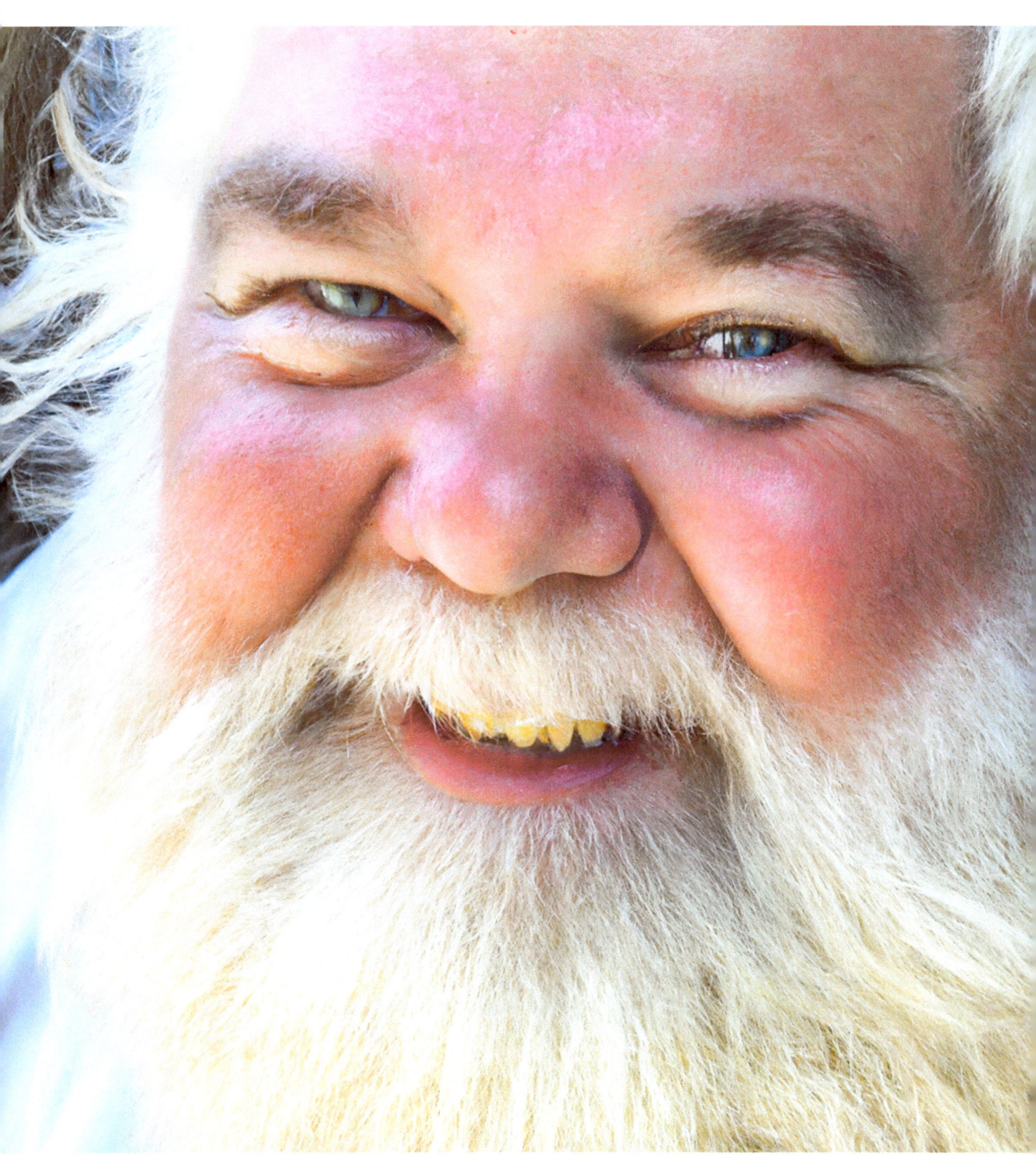

PROMPT: Closeup of a happy blue-eyed seventy year old chubby man with tousled pure white curly hair, long pure white beard, pure white bushy eyebrows and a ruddy complexion.

Inpainting edits

At this stage of the software development, the editing tool is not very refined. You can erase a blob and let the program regenerate the area. It sort of works but doesn't do a spectacular job if you want a high quality product. Most importantly you don't have much control of the tool.

The Edit tool made the Santa hat. It also made the bit of shoulder showing red and white fabric of his coat. In that case, I removed the area of the photo I wanted to replace and then typed "Dressed as Santa" in the prompt.

It took me a few tries to get white bushy eyebrows on my Santa that had brown eyebrows. The tool works well to remove blemishes or errors in the image. It is tougher to get folds of fabric smooth or to move the folds elsewhere on the figure.

The editing tool did not do a good job for me in the creation of a new background. It did not handle hair well (a true test of a digital tool). I never had the tool create better eyes than the original image. Eyeballs that were strange to start with often became stranger still after using the Edit tool.

I used Variation a lot, just to see what would happen. Most often the image just became more plastic, smoother looking. You can see in the Variation example, the bad eye became more peculiar. This is something I always fixed in Photoshop at the end.

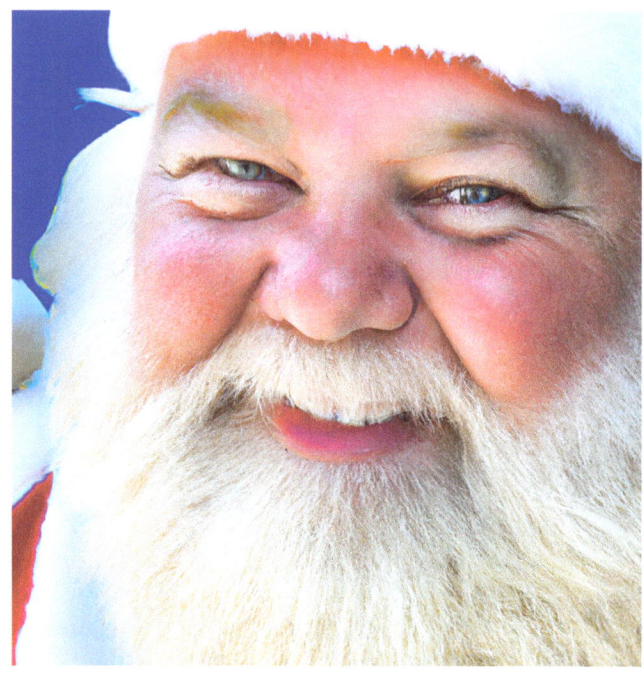

EDIT PROMPT: Blue background.

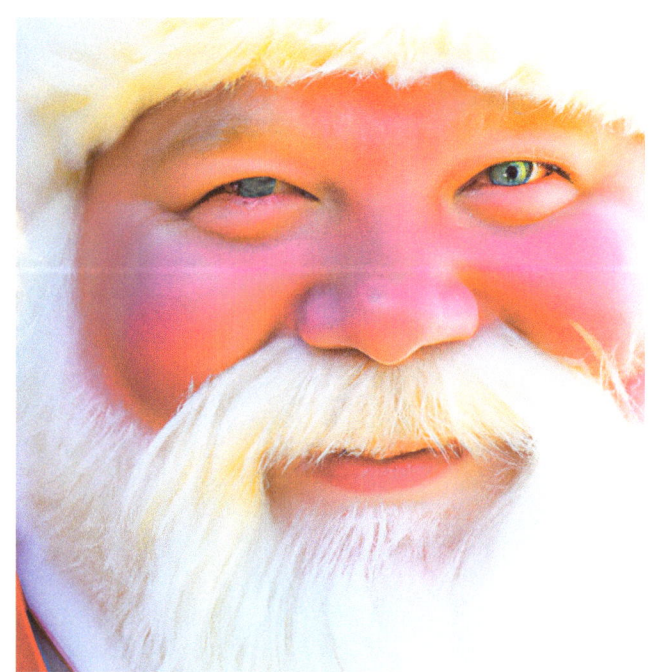

PROMPT: Variations

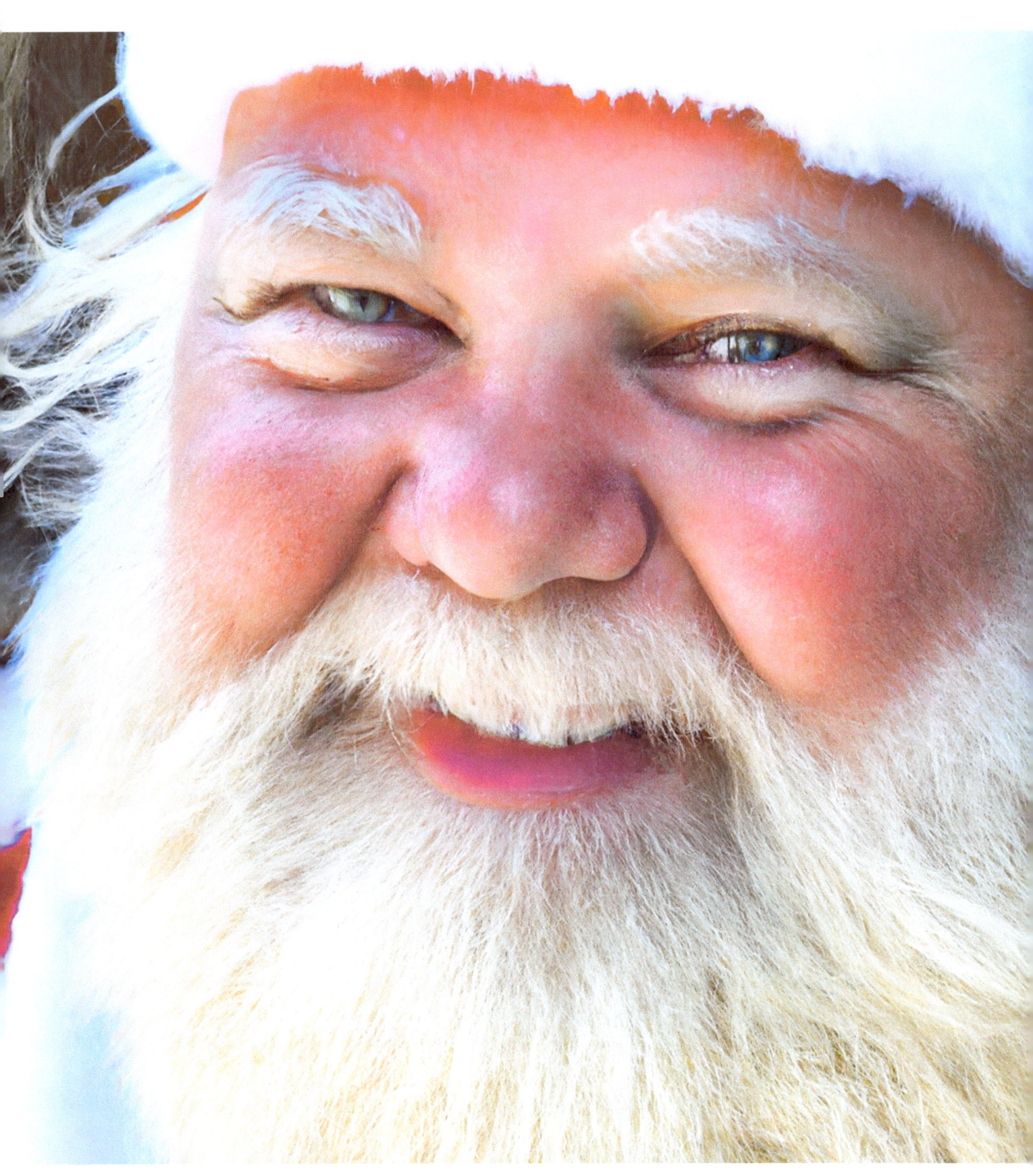

EDIT PROMPT: Dressed as Santa, EDIT PROMPT: White eyebrows

Variations

This is a fun tool. I started with a cartoony Santa photo that specified a fisheye lens. By doing several generations of Variations, the images quickly reminded me of digital animation. This is one aspect of this software, beyond creating images that would be fun to play with. Dall•E2 would be great to use for character development for either static panel or 3-D animation story-telling.

Here and on the next pages are Variations based on the original generation, *right*. Each generation lost detail and became more plastic-looking until my last Variation, *below*. To me, this Variation looks like a plastic baby toy. It's a whole other way to use Dall•E2 as part of a creative workflow.

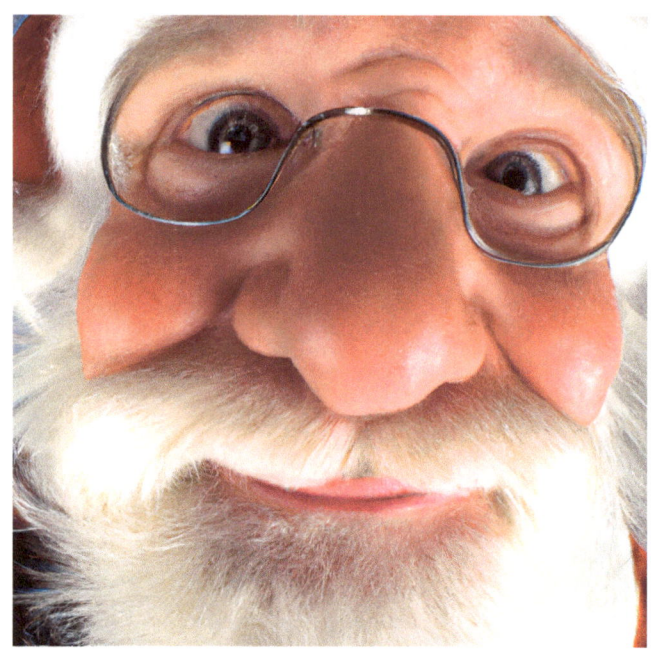

PROMPT: Happy Caucasian blue-eyed Santa closeup smiling, studio lighting, 8k, fisheye lens.

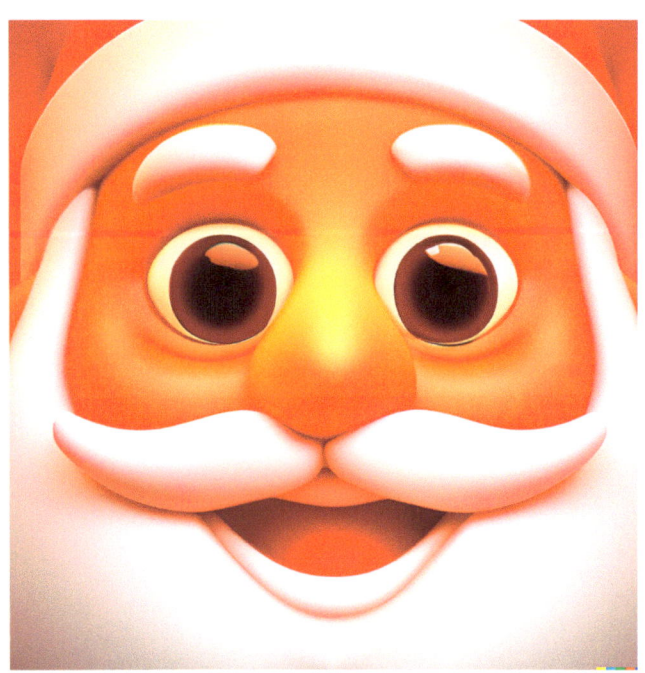

PROMPT: Variations

PROMPT: Variations

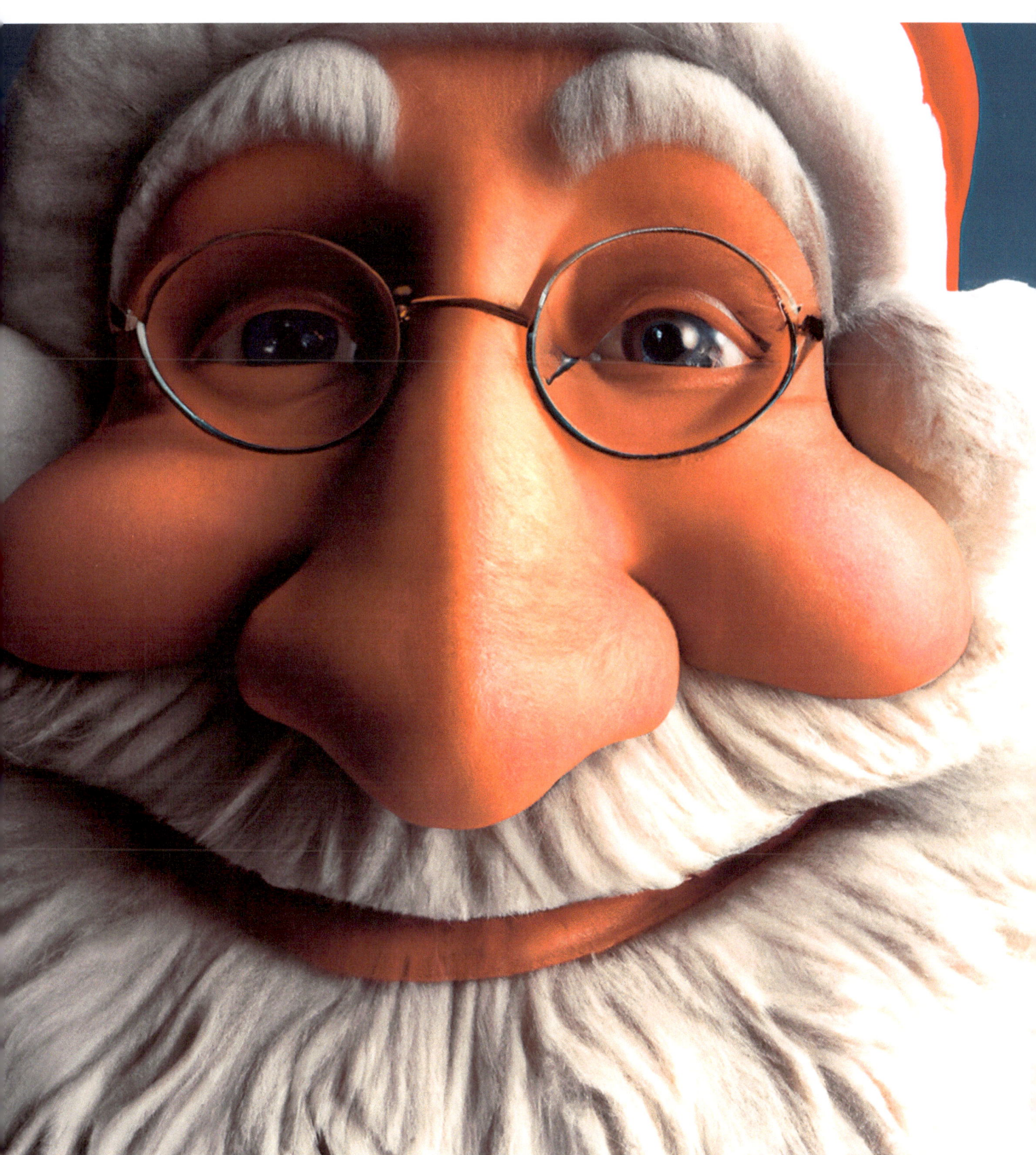

PROMPT: Variations

Variations: series

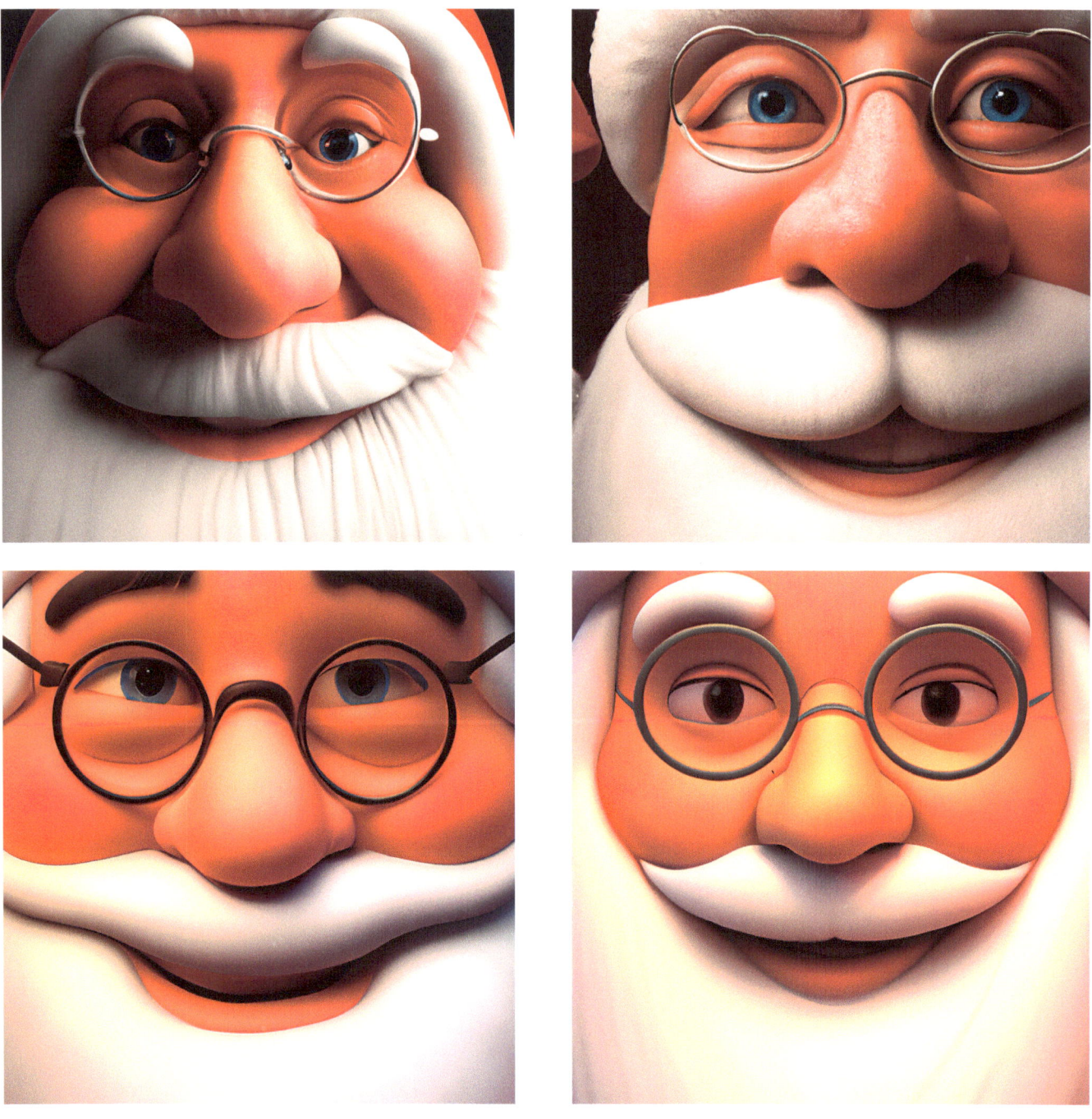

18 MAKING SANTA

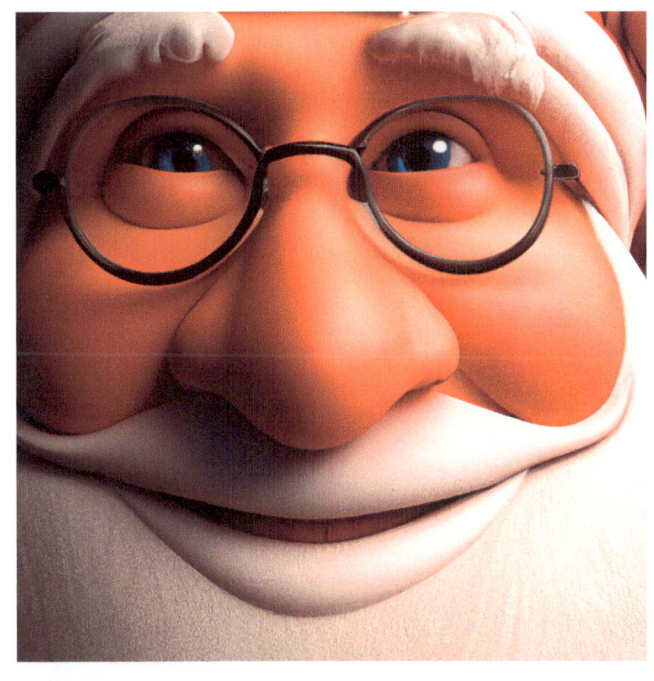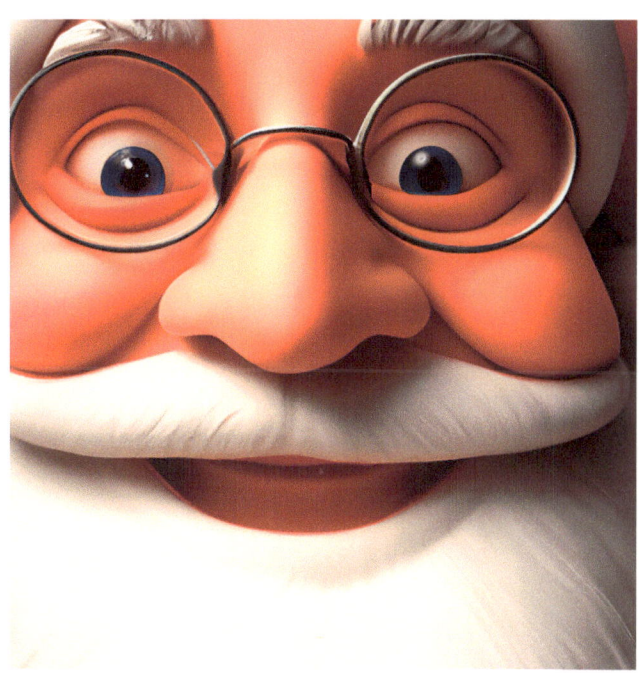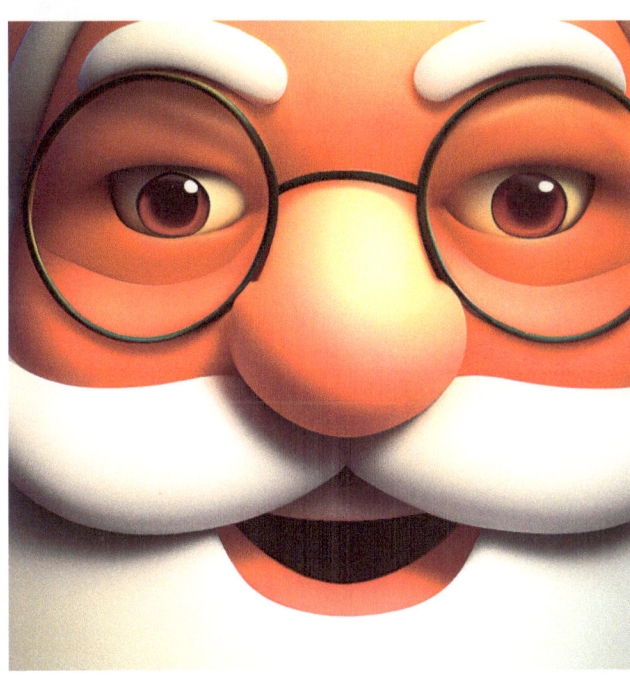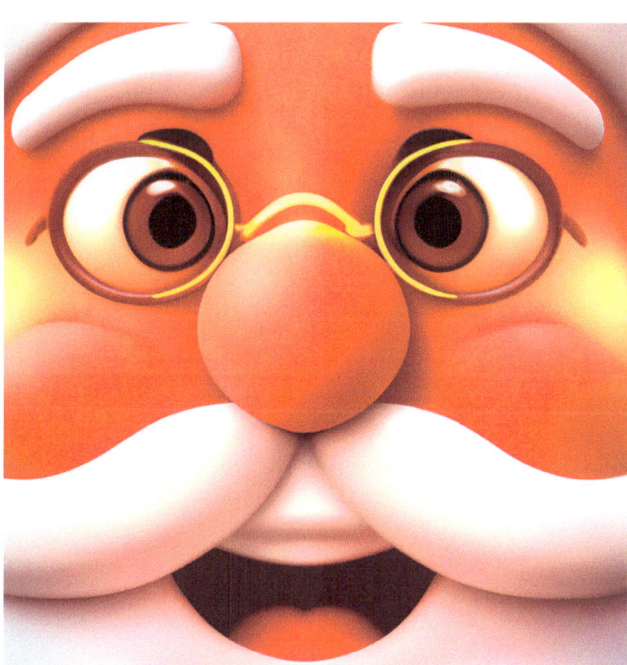

External software edits

I routinely repaired Dall•E2 generated eyeballs and teeth in Photoshop. My typical process was to replace the iris, replace or create the pupil and then add light highlights. I like one white dot in the eyes. Often the eyeballs were two different sizes. Sometimes the structure of the eye was odd and needed to be corrected. In this image the eyelid had a strange texture and color that needed to be smoothed out.

Eyes are a critical part of a photographic-style image and need to be right for the viewer to connect with the character. An untrained eye might not know what was wrong with an eye but they would instinctively feel like something was not right. I also routinely whitened yellow teeth, removed extra rows of teeth and repaired broken teeth.

Since the images were being prepped for publication, they often needed to be in a vertical or horizontal format—so more background was needed or in the case of Santa, more hat. The Dall•E2 tool didn't do a good job of replacing background around hair or fur, so I did that manually. Changing the background was done in Photoshop using color, filters for texture, paintbrush, eraser and blur.

Right top, original eye. *Right bottom*, repaired eye. *Next page*, background added and more hat added.

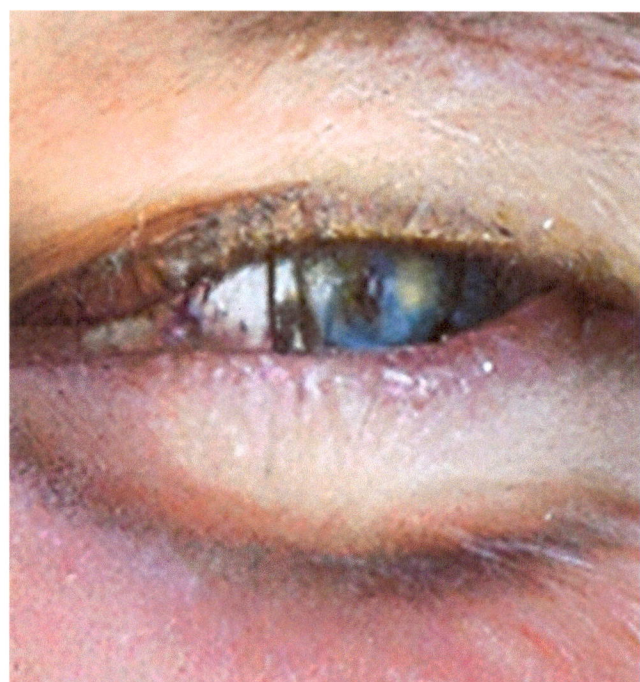

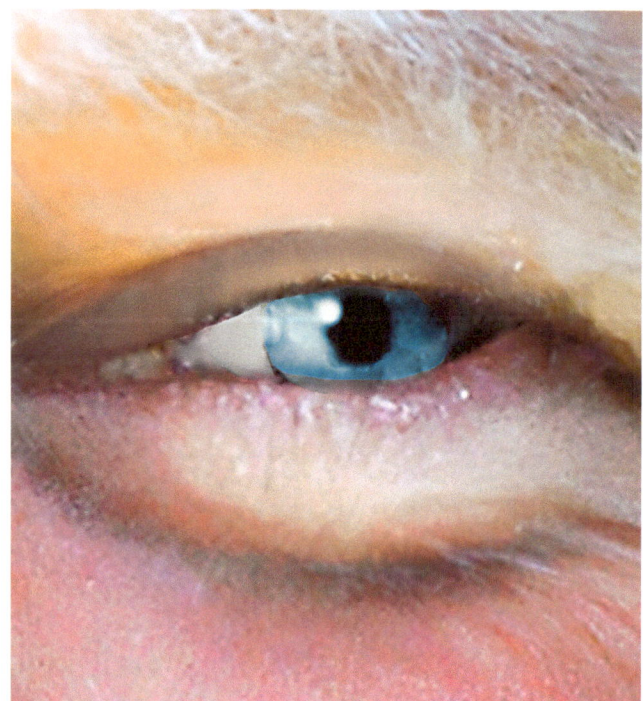

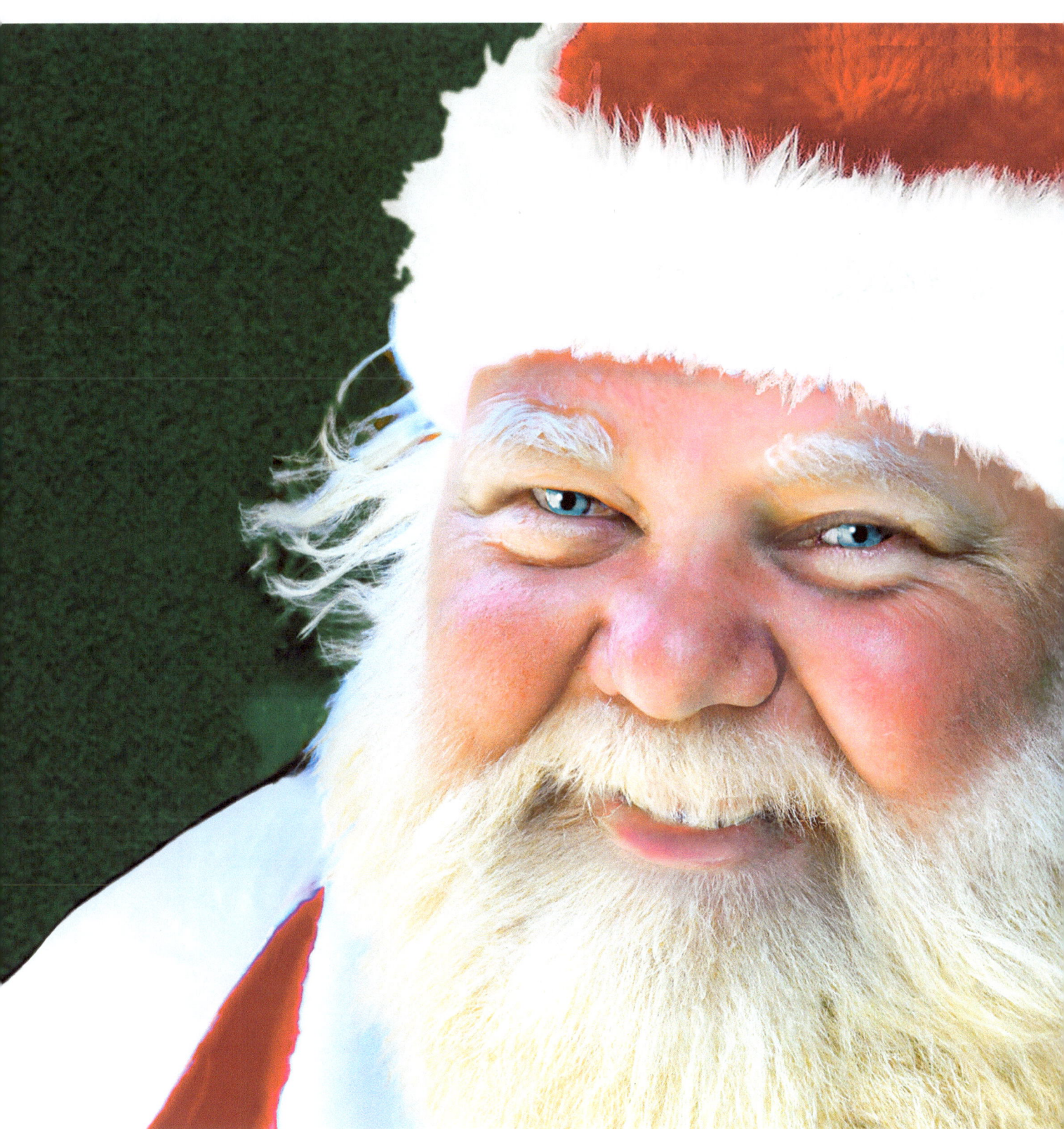

Full figure Santa

I had trouble getting a full head-to-toe photographic image of a Santa. When I tried prompts using those terms I received cut off heads, no feet. The more body I acquired, the lower the quality of the rendering—especially the facial features. I finally got one full figure. Then I did one edit to try and get a better face. It still needs a lot of work. His belt doesn't go all the way around the body. The quality of the face rendering is poor and his posture and expression looks more crabby than jolly.

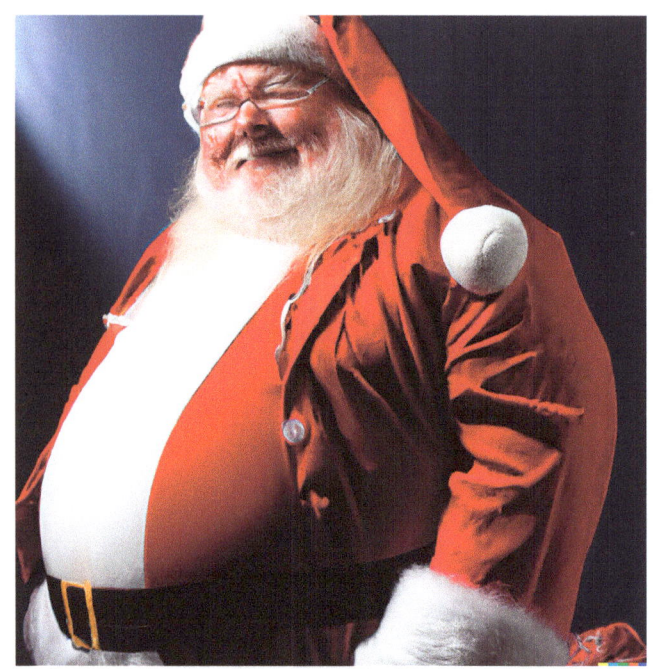

PROMPT: Dramatic studio lighting high-resolution photo of a plump, rosy-cheeked, blue-eyed, jolly old man with a white beard, round belly and red suit.

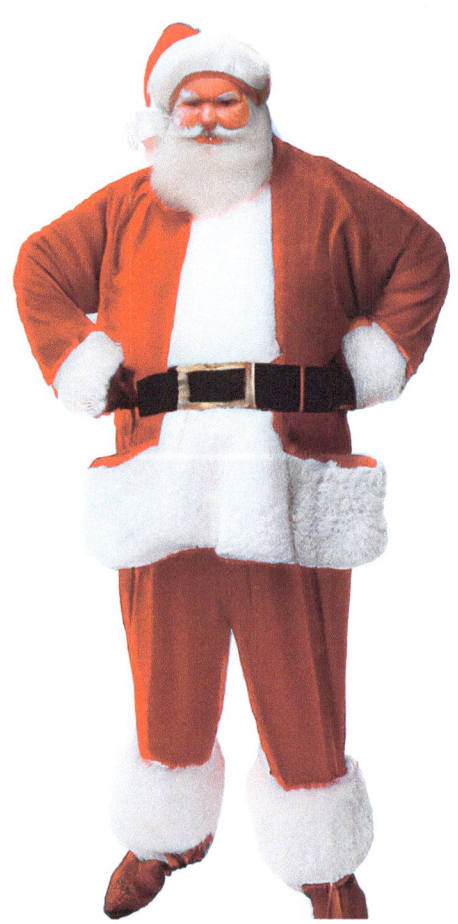

PROMPT: Full-length, wide shot, rosy-cheeked, jolly old man dressed in a red suit, white beard, smiling.

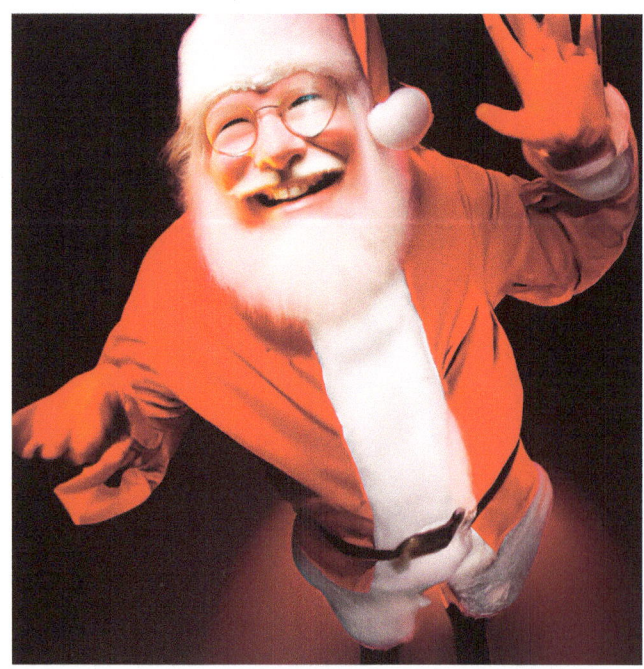

PROMPT: Wide angle studio lighting of a jolly old man, white beard, round belly and red suit.
EDIT PROMPT: Smiling, happy.

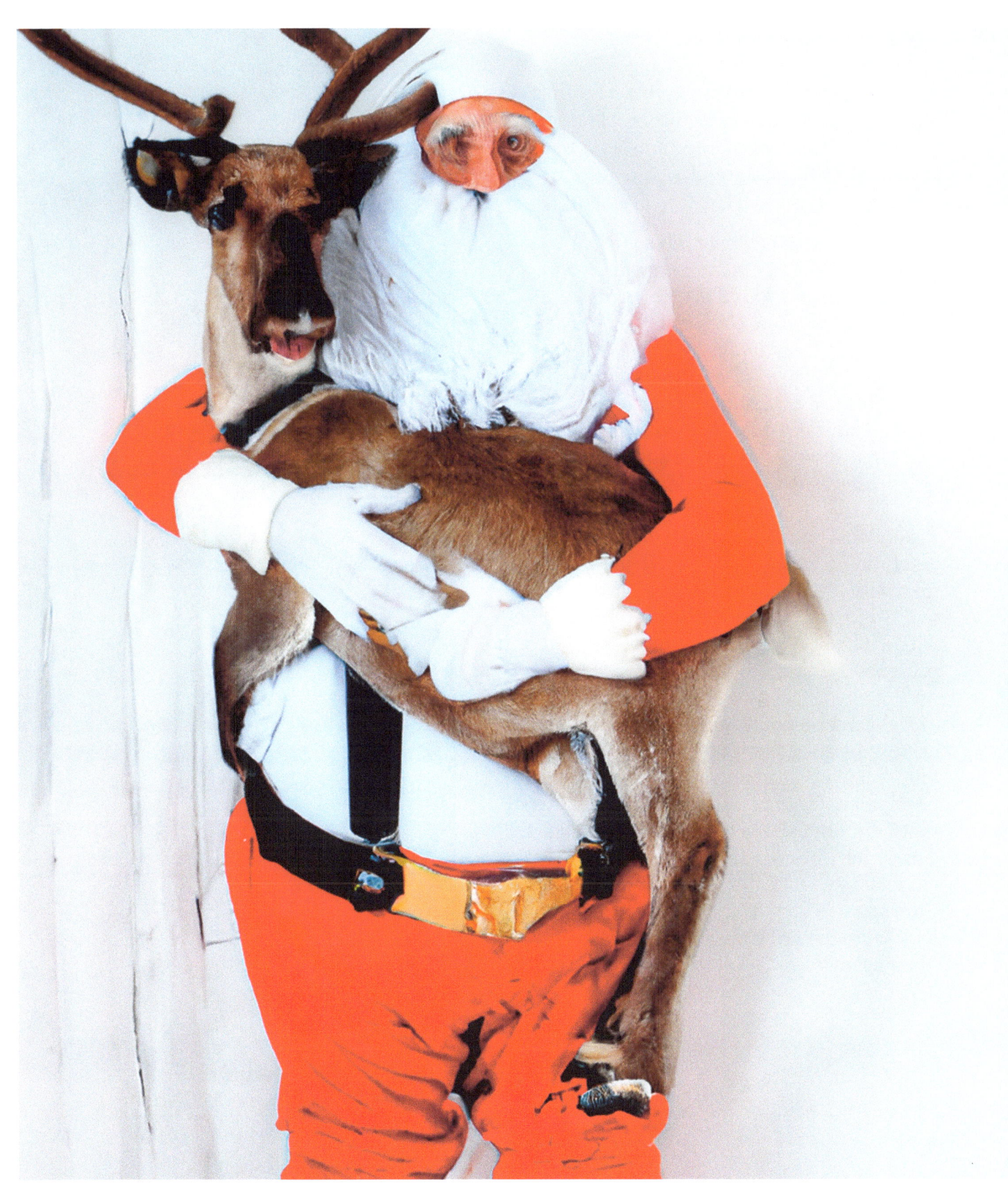

PROMPT: Photo of Santa in red pants and suspenders hugging a reindeer.

Another prompt strategy

Instead of trying to guess what AI thinks Santa looks like, ask it. My prompt for ChatGPT was simple, "Describe Santa Claus." It returned this paragraph:

> *Santa Claus is a fictional character who is said to deliver presents to children around the world on Christmas Eve. He is usually depicted as a jolly, rotund man with a white beard, dressed in a red suit with white fur trim, black boots, and a red hat with a white pom-pom. He is often shown carrying a sack full of presents over his shoulder...*

PROMPT: Dramatic studio lighting high-resolution portrait of blue-eyed, jolly, rotund man with a white beard, dressed in a red suit with white fur trim, black boots, and a red hat with a white pom-pom carrying a sack full of presents over his shoulder, 8k.

Dalle•E2 returned Santa images. I never achieved a good face on a full-length figure, but I got good headshots and can cut and paste later. The interesting thing to me was that I did not use the word Santa, but Dall•E2 clearly returned Santa. The images and characters were realistic and photographic. Editing them as Variations moved the graphic look more toward a more plastic digital imaging style.

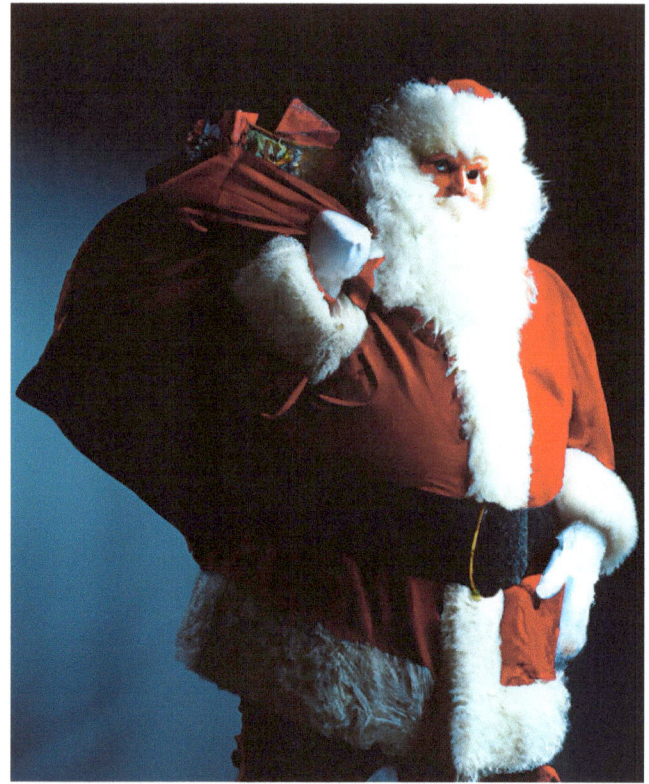

PROMPT: See left

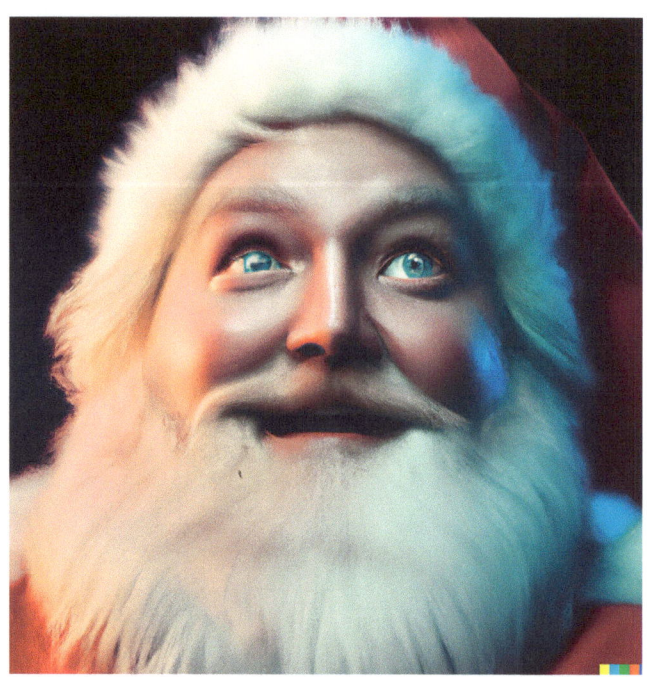

PROMPT: Variation

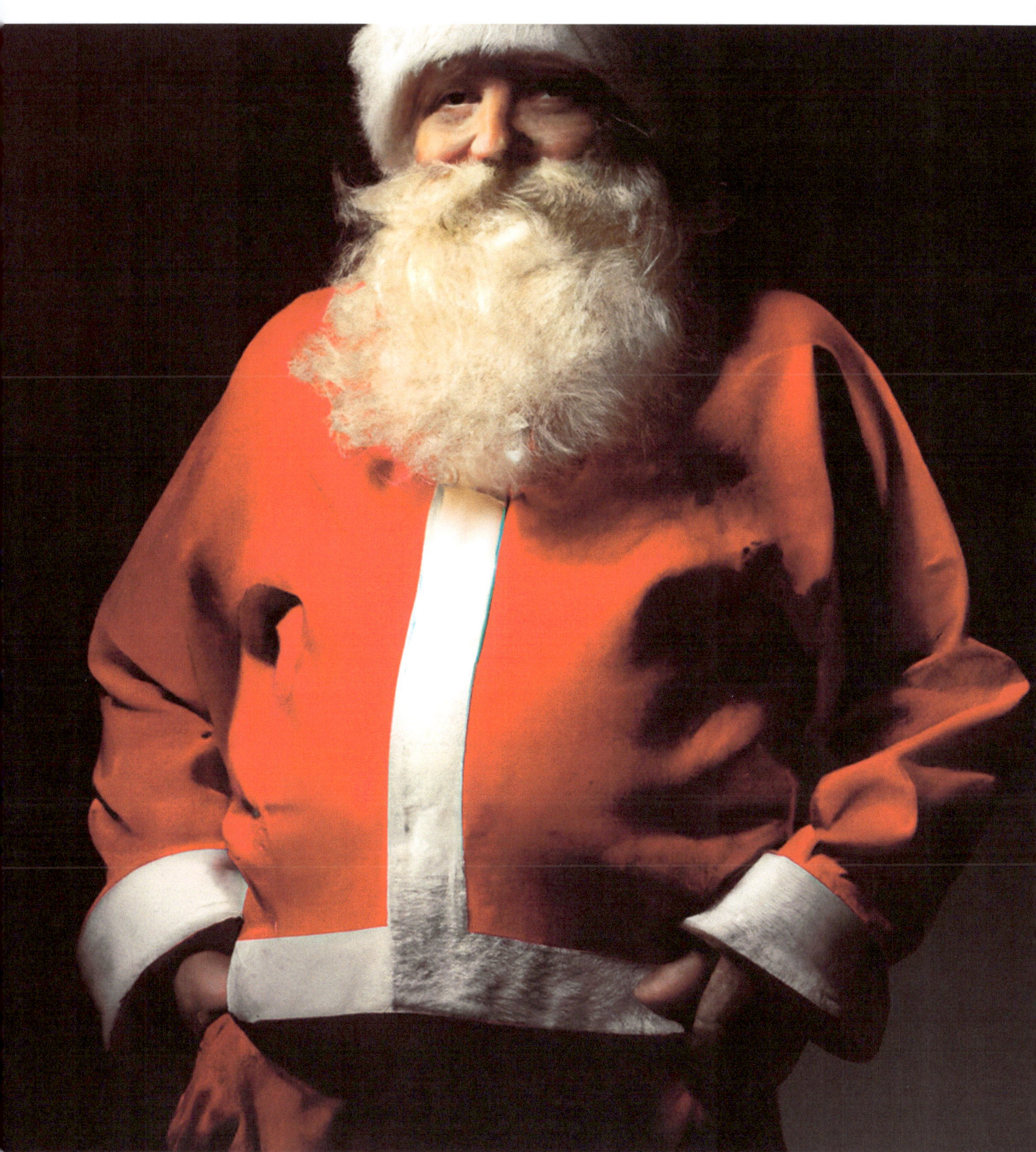

PROMPT: Dramatic studio lighting high-resolution photo of a plump, rosy-cheeked, jolly old man with a white beard, round belly and red suit.

Outpainting vs Photoshop

Dall•E2 Outpainting and Photoshop Content-Aware Fill are very similar. I tried them both on this image of "Santa" with walking sticks in the woods with a reindeer. I wanted more of the environment around the figures so they were smaller in proportion to the frame.

With the Dall•2 tool, *below*, I got a lot of unwanted digital artifacts and didn't have any control except to select a block to expand the background. I was much happier with Photoshop to accomplish my goal here. I was able to make shaped selections as well as replicate specific areas of the image.

I am sure the Dall•E2 tools will improve with every release. I didn't find Outpainting effective in this one test. Photoshop did the same process but was a little more successful in how it built out the image.

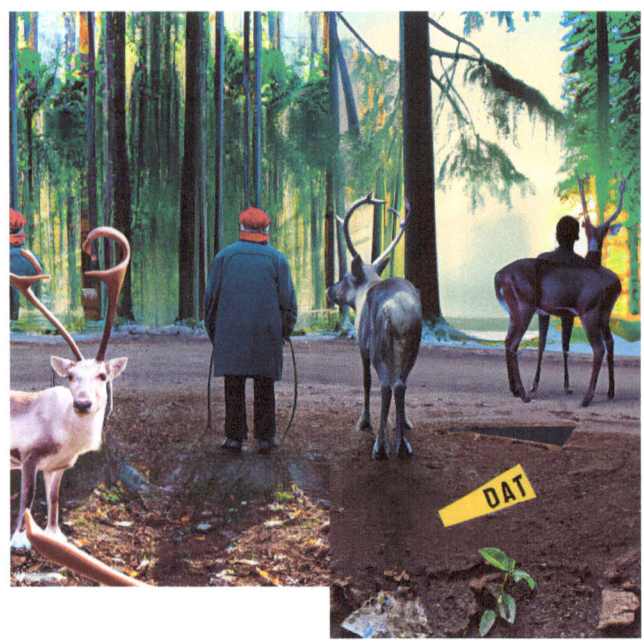

Results using DALL•E2 Outpainting

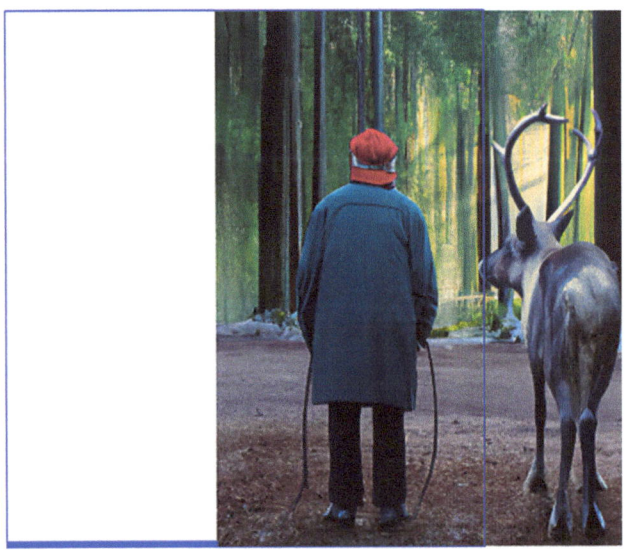

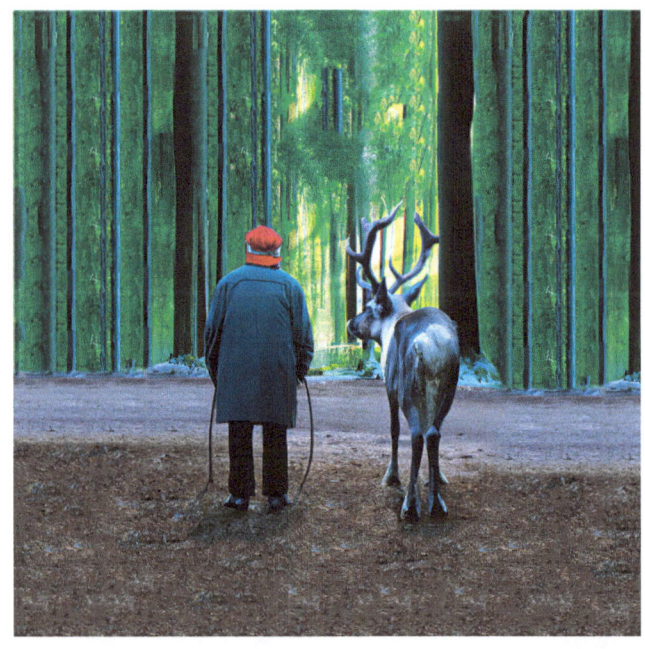

Results using Photoshop Content-Aware Fill

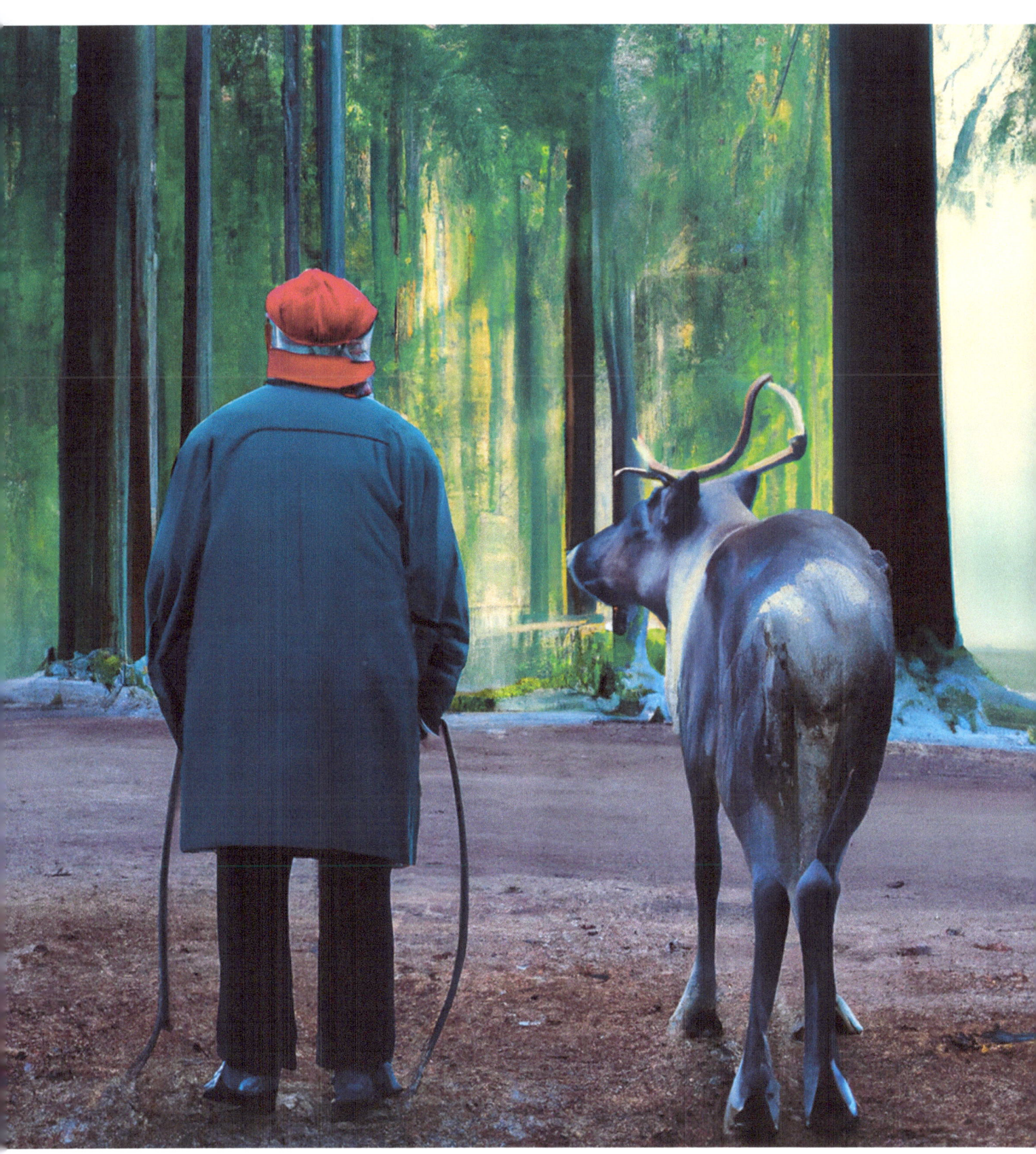

PROMPT: Photo of the full figure of an old man in the woods from behind standing next to a reindeer. A Variation resulted in the corrected antlers, red and green outfit.

Prep for printing or digital distribution

The Dall•E2 images were PNG files with a resolution of 72 ppi. The pixel dimensions of the file were 1024 square. I opened each file in Photoshop and saved it as a PSD file. I changed the pixel dimensions to 1728 pixels square and 300 ppi. In the case of the cover, I work the file at 600 ppi.

The original file was also in RGB color format, which at some point I had to convert to CMYK to get a more accurate read on how it would print. Color corrections and retouching were done in CMYK, usually a flat file—layers were flattened.

Layouts were done in Adobe InDesign and images were positioned from PSD files. Once the layout was finalized, the images were sized, saved and re-placed in the layout from flat PSD files at 300 ppi and 100% size.

The final cover was saved to a PDF with a resolution of 300 ppi. The body of the document was also saved as a PDF with a resolution of 300 ppi. For digital distribution, both the cover and the body were flattened, reduced to 96 ppi and optimized to reduce file size as a PDF.

Interestingly, Amazon flagged the Dall•E2 logo as production bars and requested they be removed. So each full image, at some point in the production process, had the color bar logo removed. I would have been happy to leave it in, but Amazon stopped the document in the process until they were removed. Also because of Amazon specifications, the final images printed were saved down to 200 ppi. Amazon limits manuscript file size.

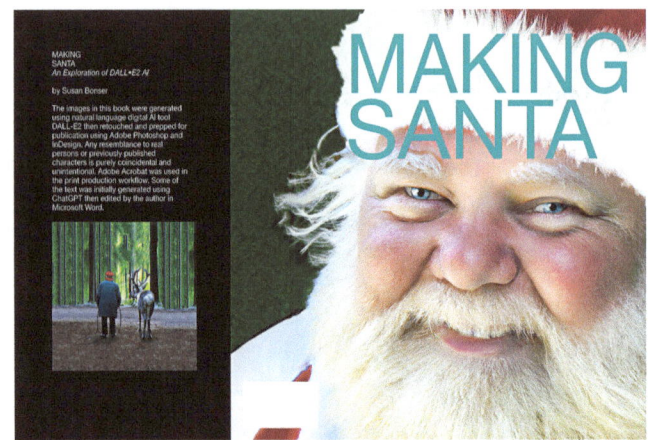

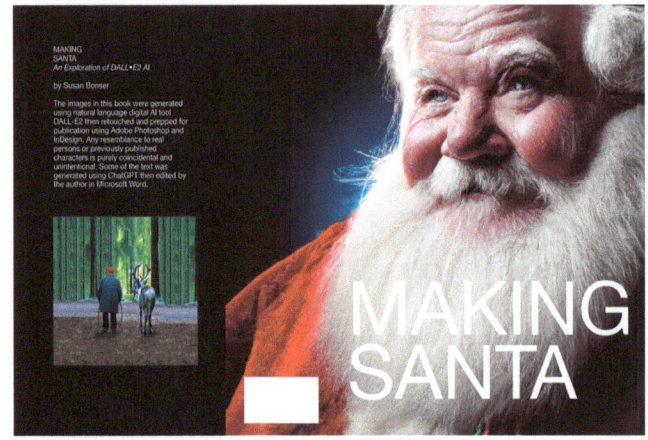

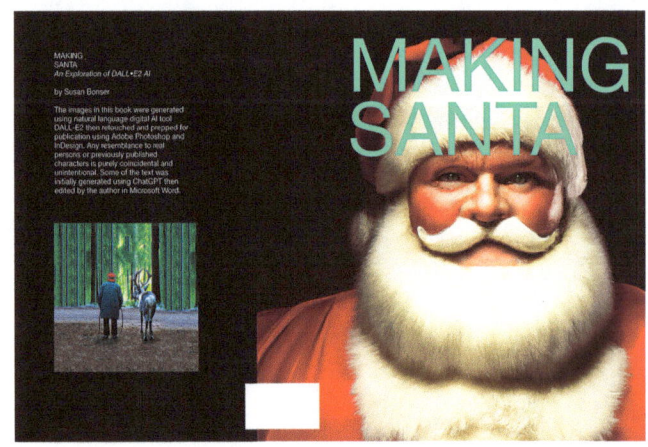

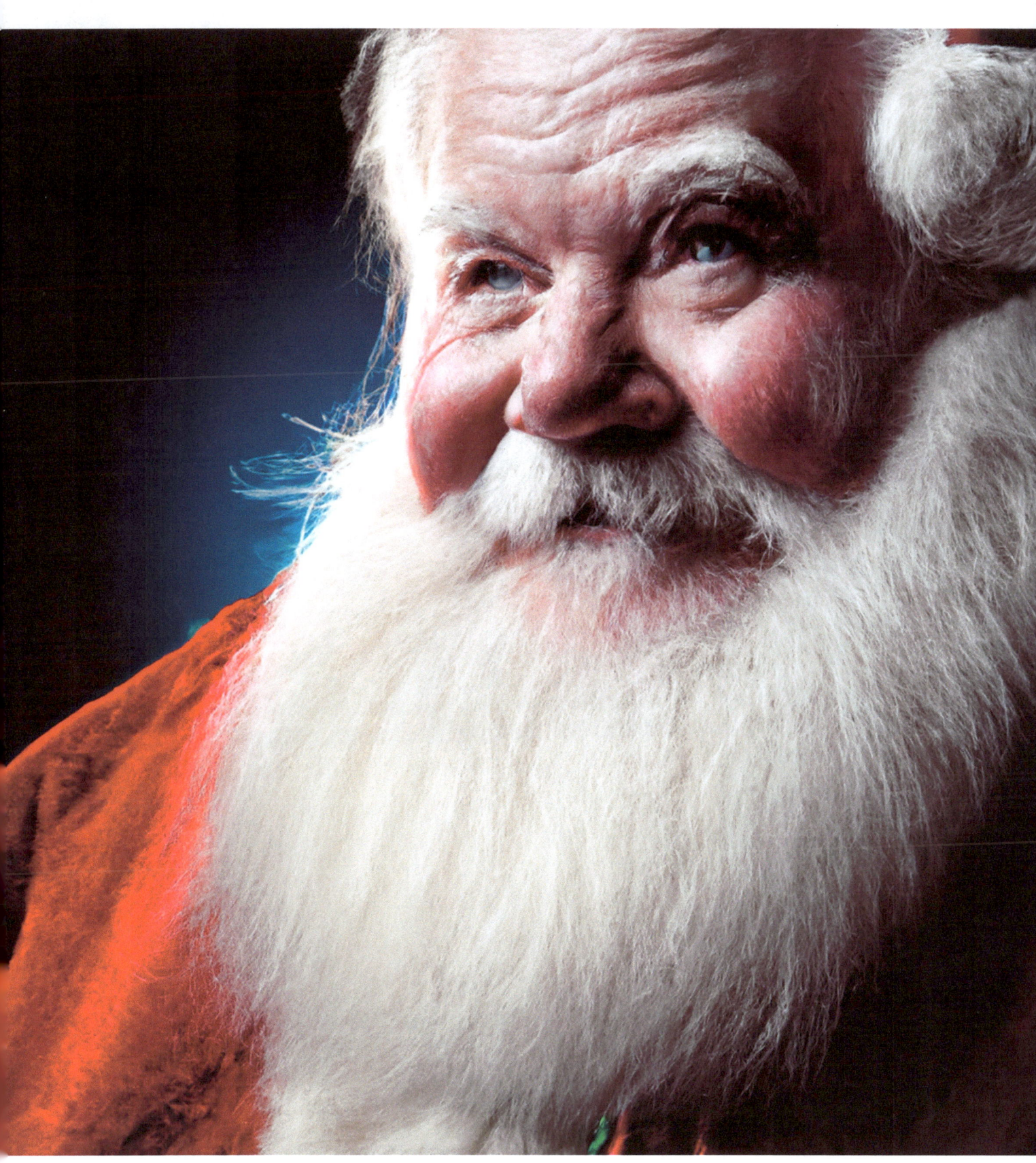

PROMPT: Dramatic studio lighting high resolution photo of a plump, rosy-cheeked, blue-eyed, jolly old man with a white beard, round belly and red suit.

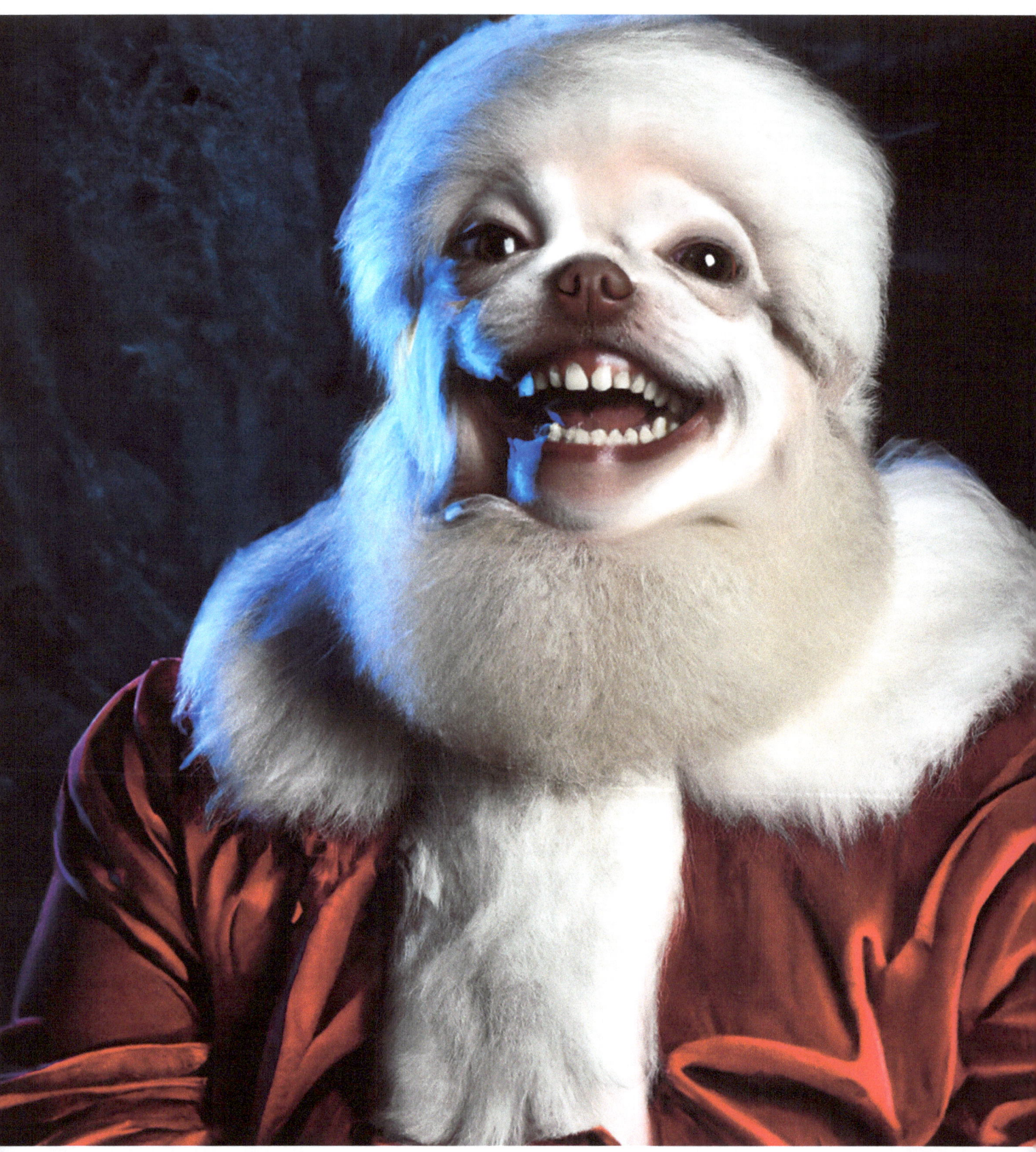

Prompt: Smiling, happy.
In this case, with the original prompt removed and the simple prompt above, the program chose to make dog and monkey-faced Santas. Oops.

www.ingramcontent.com/pod-product-compliance
Lightning Source LLC
Chambersburg PA
CBHW051827210526
45473CB00005B/1773